Heaven's Gate: The History and Legacy of Marshall Applewhite's Notorious Doomsday Cult

By Charles River Editors

Comet Hale-Bopp

About Charles River Editors

Charles River Editors provides superior editing and original writing services across the digital publishing industry, with the expertise to create digital content for publishers across a vast range of subject matter. In addition to providing original digital content for third party publishers, we also republish civilization's greatest literary works, bringing them to new generations of readers via ebooks.

Sign up here to receive updates about free books as we publish them, and visit Our Kindle Author Page to browse today's free promotions and our most recently published Kindle titles.

Introduction

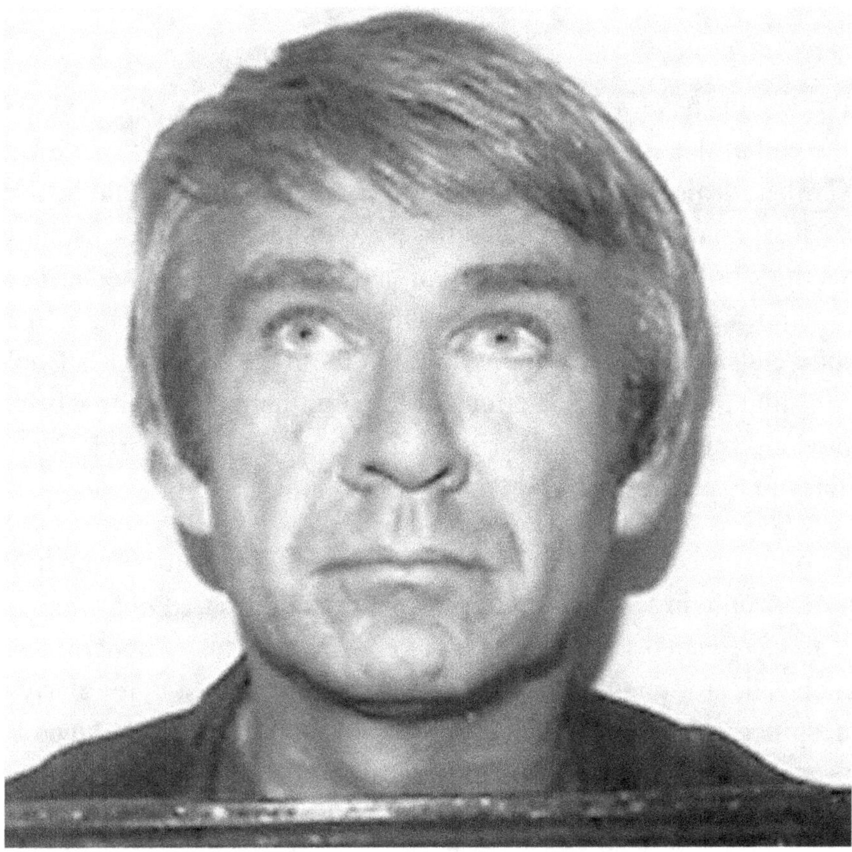

Applewhite's mugshot in 1974

"Hale–Bopp brings closure to Heaven's Gate ... Our 22 years of classroom here on planet Earth is finally coming to conclusion—'graduation' from the Human Evolutionary Level. We are happily prepared to leave 'this world' and go with Ti's crew."

To most people, it is almost impossible to understand the mere existence, let alone the baffling, yet indubitable appeal of doomsday cults, but they have been morbidly fascinating phenomena throughout history.

One such recent cult is the infamous Chinese quasi-Christian subgroup Eastern Lightning, also known as the "Church of the Almighty God," founded in 1991 and officially banned in 1995. Apart from its peculiar dogma that Jesus Christ has returned to Earth in the form of a Chinese woman and its involvement in multiple crimes and controversies, including alleged mass kidnappings and the murder of a 37-year-old saleswoman, its members were some of the most aggressive proponents of the Mayan doomsday theory, which predicted the end of the world on December 21, 2012. But doomsday cults are far older than most would imagine. Montanism, another Christian offshoot, was established by the exclusive channeler of the Paraclete (the Biblical Spirit of Truth), Montanus, in Phrygia in the 2nd century CE. In its time, hundreds, if not thousands of Christian villagers relinquished their homes and belongings to congregate at a rolling plain between the villages of Tymion and Pepuza, where they awaited the second coming of Christ.

Not all apocalyptic cults have waited for the anti-climactic finales of their failed doomsday prophecies. At the end of the 19th century, one of the major evangelists in the United States preached his revivalist ideals and started a wave of evangelism that would last well into the 20th century. Dwight Moody, an American evangelist who founded the Moody Church, deplored the new scholarly readings of the Bible, the theory of evolution, and preached a literal second coming of Christ happening soon. Moody's fundamentalism produced energetic reactions from various apocalyptic cults, and many of them found in the New Testament's Book of Revelation their reason for existing and their expectations of the imminent end of the world. In some cases, these cults tried to help bring it about, figuring that if the end of the world didn't arrive on its own, they would try to usher it in themselves.

The bizarre and often objectively comical beliefs of these offbeat denominations are so far removed from most people in society that even the horrific fates that befell the devoted disciples of the latter cults have repeatedly been reduced to cheap, throwaway punchlines. The phrase "drinking the Kool-Aid," for one, has become an overused expression regularly tossed around in playful banter, despite the fact it is a derogatory reference to the cyanide-laced Flavor-Aid ingested by 908 members (many of them children) of the Peoples Temple cult in Jonestown, Guyana at the behest of their leader, Reverend Jim Jones, in 1978.

David Koresh, leader of the Branch Davidians, had deep convictions based on the Book of Daniel and the Book of Revelation, and his sect believed the world was in the power of Satan and that the nations were merging to form a new Babylon. David hoped to establish the kingdom in Jerusalem, where, according to him, he would suffer martyrdom. The headquarters of the sect was a complex called Mount Carmel Center located in Waco, Texas. In the last manuscript produced by Koresh, which was preserved by a woman named Ruth Riddle who escaped the fire, the cult leader spoke extensively about his identity and the mystery of the Seven Seals. Koresh claimed to be the mysterious Lamb of Revelation who opens the sealed scroll, as well as the figure who rides the White Horse when the first seal is opened.

While Waco remains notorious more for the federal agents' siege of Koresh's compound and the deaths of the Branch Davidians, it was followed a few years later by a mass suicide carried out by one of the most notorious doomsday cults in American history. On paper, the extraordinarily unorthodox ideology spouted by Heaven's Gate ranks near the top of the list of most outlandish end-of-the-world prophecies, and it was built on a blend of Christian, Gnostic, supernatural, New Age, and extraterrestrial lore. Although the cult did not speak in Christian terms, it was clearly apocalyptic, and its belief system was a strange mix between science fiction and the basic message of Revelation. The cult's leader, Marshall Applewhite, and his female companion, Bonnie Nettles, concluded that they were the two witnesses mentioned in Revelation 11:3-4: "And I will give power to my two witnesses, and they will prophesy one thousand two hundred and sixty days, clothed in sackcloth. These are the two olive trees and the two lampstands standing before the God of the Earth."

Applewhite believed the Earth would be transformed and renewed, and that evil entities (not beasts, but in this case, aliens) called Luciferans conspired against humanity. In his view, the elect members of Heaven's Gate would be taken up to a spaceship when the hour came. The opportunity to join the Rapture arrived with the passing of comet Hale-Bopp in 1997. Applewhite told his congregation that a spaceship was following the comet, and that the event would mark the closure of the gates of Heaven, making the spaceship the last opportunity to leave Earth. Over the course of three days, 39 members committed ritual mass suicide, all dressed identically, to be taken up by the UFO.

Heaven's Gate: The History and Legacy of Marshall Applewhite's Notorious Doomsday Cult chronicles the notorious cult and the mass suicide. Along with pictures of important people, places, and events, you will learn about Heaven's Gate like never before.

When Two Become One

On the third week of March in 1997, dozens of curious looking, modestly dressed individuals sporting similar cropped and buzzed haircuts gathered at a sunlit and verdant California glade. The group took turns – some in pairs, some in threes, and some opting to tackle the task individually – plopping down on the plastic chairs set up in front of a camcorder on a tripod, which they had brought with them, and proceeded to film a series of five-minute segments. To the casual eye, these recordings seem like wholesome, albeit dull content, such as a well-intentioned, but forgettable promotional tourism video, or perhaps even a cheesy video dating montage from some obscure rural town. When viewers learn the true context behind the videos, however, which range from unfocused and long-winded off-the-cuff monologues punctuated by addled pauses to pre-prepared statements, the videos become far more chilling, because these outwardly lighthearted recordings are none other than the video manifestos, or "exit videos," taped by 38 members of the Heaven's Gate cult about a week prior to their mass suicide, which would turn the worlds of their surviving loved ones upside down and leave the rest of the world disturbed and shocked beyond belief.

For each segment, an off-screen videographer asked the subjects to introduce themselves, including the date of their enrollment, before sharing their last words. One video features a pair of young men – one clad in a peach button-down and the other in a navy-blue track jacket – who call themselves "QSTODY" and "SRRODY," respectively. SRRODY, who joined the cult on Valentine's Day in 1976, appears almost giddy, giggling and restlessly gesturing with his hands as he launches into his segment: "Oh goodness, there is so much I want to say to you...I would really strongly recommend if you can find Heaven's Gate – the book, the website...it'll do you a lot of good...You're better off trusting that than whatever information you come across on TV..." He then addressed friends and former members who had made repeated attempts to warn him about his newfound family before the videographer instructs him to express his thoughts on how he feels about the group's impending "exit": "This is the happiest day of my life. I've been looking forward to this for so long...Somebody watching this would probably say...'You're deluded or you're brainwashed'...[but] from my perspective, this is...the answer to everything. These flesh vehicles – if you use the analogy of a car...some people say here's a newer model of a car, it's much nicer...this [old] model doesn't quite perform the way it could, so I'd like to move into this new car...That's about all we're talking about; it's not a big deal..."

A second clip features a pair of middle-age women, garbed in checkered and lapis-blue button-downs, who refer to themselves as "LVVODY" and "JNNODY." Unlike QSTODY and SRRODY, the ladies struggle to make prolonged eye contact with the camera, and their seemingly forced, tight-lipped smiles are unsettling, to say the least. LVVODY, the first to speak, is visibly overcome with emotion, with tears welling up in her eyes and her voice cracking every few seconds. "We're very happy and proud to have been members of Ti and Do's class, and couldn't be happier about what we're about to do," LVVODY stammers, taking a deep breath to compose herself. Peals of encouraging laughter can be heard in the background. "That was never an issue. Certainly, at times, temptations of the vehicle...some influences may turn our heads this way or that...[but] there's always a deep down knowing that the moment of seeing Ti and Do...this is why I'm here to do this task..."

The bespectacled QSTODY chimes in, "Probably...the blame will be pointed at Ti and Do...[but] we've always had free reign to come and go, to believe or not believe since day one in the class...Ti and Do would make an effort to push anyone out of the class who didn't want to be here...The more we put into practice – the teachings, the behavior, and the guidelines – the truth that they held becomes more apparent...The last thing that I would've thought on September 13th, 1975 is that in a week, I would find myself in a group leaving behind my human life...but there was just a knowing and a recognition that...Ti and Do were someone [sic] that I had known prior to this reincarnation..."

LVVODY concludes their joint statement: "I can't help but think of the Bible, when Jesus says 'I am the way and the truth and life. No one comes to Father except through me,' he was saying, 'I'm here, I'm sent, the Kingdom of Heaven is at hand. I am the only way you can reach the Next Level of the Kingdom of Heaven.' Now it's the end of the age...and Ti and Do are the Way and the Truth, and the only source of life, and without our connection to Ti and Do, we have nothing..."

From an outsider's perspective, these farewell video diaries are surreal, and they are concrete proof of what can happen when lost, troubled souls are led astray by the illusory promises and specious guidance of deranged individuals. But to achieve a better understanding of why the doomed disciples of Heaven's Gate – previously known as the Next Level Crew, Total Overcomers Anonymous, and the Human Individual Metamorphosis – so willingly submitted themselves to such a cause, it's necessary to look at the lives of the cult's founders and the genesis of the Next Level movement.

Marshall Herff Applewhite was born on March 17, 1931 in the small city of Spur, Texas, situated about 325 miles northwest of Austin. He was the son of Texan natives Marshall Herff Applewhite Sr., a roving Presbyterian pastor, and his 30-year-old wife, Louise Haecker Winfield. Marshall had two older sisters named Louise and Jane, as well as a severely physically and mentally challenged younger brother named John, who was later sent to live in a state-run assisted living facility in the city.

While Applewhite grew up comfortably in a middle-class household, he learned from a young age to never become overly attached to his friends and surroundings because his father's job required constant relocation. Every three years or so, the family uprooted to various towns and cities of varying sizes throughout southern Texas, which included places such as Roscoe, Sweetwater, Corpus Christi, and San Antonio. Nevertheless, Applewhite appeared to be a happy-go-lucky and well-adjusted child, with his dirty-blond hair always impeccably gelled. He was often seen with an extra bounce in his step and a permanent twinkle in his cornflower-blue eyes.

By most accounts, Applewhite, Sr. seemed to have been a stellar role model. He was a solid, family-oriented man who never hesitated to help out the community, in particular when it came to constructing churches and assembling congregations from scratch in every town and city on his route. In a later interview, Floyd Chapman, president of the Corpus Christi Electric Company, recounted his experiences with Applewhite, Sr., who built and presided over the Parkway Presbyterian Church in the early 1950s. Chapman described the minister as a jovial man with exceptional organizational and leadership skills "who built [the] church up to a couple of hundred members pretty [quickly]." He further commended Applewhite, Sr. and his wife, who served as the church's choir director and resident organ player, for their children's excellent manners.

That said, according to one conflicting account, which came from an unnamed family friend, how Applewhite, Sr. behaved behind closed doors was apparently a very different story. Applewhite, Sr. is said to have been a strict, "terribly authoritative," and rigidly stubborn man, and he was especially hard on his only son and namesake, so much so that the family friend found it to be a cause for concern. Either way, young Marshall admired his father profoundly and wanted nothing more than to make him proud.

There were virtually no signs from Applewhite's youth that foretold his harrowing future, apart from his competitive nature. He was an ambitious go-getter who brimmed with personality and enlisted in several extracurricular clubs and student councils. He also competed for the presidential posts in these organizations. "He was always a born leader and very charismatic," said his sister Louise. "He could get people to believe anything."

Following his graduation from Corpus Christi High School in 1948, Applewhite went to Austin College, but what degree he pursued remains unclear. According to one account, he was listed as a philosophy major, and according to another, he double majored in Music and Pre-Theology at his father's request. He is also believed to have studied music at the University of Colorado for a semester or two, though how this fit into the timeline of his post-secondary education is also unclear.

Like those who knew Applewhite in his childhood, his peers at Austin College only had fond memories of him. He was a typical, easy-going freshman with a penchant for colorful beanies, who preferred to be referred to by his unique middle name. His roommate, John Alexander, described him as a studious extrovert, one well-liked by both teachers and classmates. "He was popular," Alexander recalled. "He was very smart, and not pushy." Moreover, he headed the judiciary council, acapella choir, and the association of Presbyterian ministers in-the-making. Despite his involvement in many of the campus' Christian clubs, Alexander insisted that Applewhite was never "fanatically religious."

Glen Maxwell, a philosophy instructor, was said to have been Applewhite's favorite professor. In addition to introducing Applewhite to Aristotle, Plato, John Locke, and other famous philosophers, Maxwell urged his students to question everything around them. He instilled in them the importance of conducting their own research and seeking answers themselves, and he assured pupils that there was no shame in swimming against the tide when it came to defending their convictions. These exhortations struck a chord with Applewhite and most likely fueled what would become his train of independent thought.

Applewhite was clearly a very bright young man of many talents, one abounding with promise. The diligence he exhibited in his academics, as well as his extensive involvement in various student societies aside, he was musically gifted and a brilliant orator, effortlessly commanding any stage he graced. He had a passion for opera, but he could hold his own in any genre, including gospels, classical numbers, or show tunes, thanks to his fine elocution and powerful baritone, which was as silvery as it was versatile. He performed in multiple stage productions and was often cast in starring or major supporting roles, such as *Annie Get Your Gun, South Pacific,* and *Oklahoma.*

Applewhite was awarded his bachelor's diploma from Austin College in 1952. Later that year, he married Ann Frances Pearce, another Texan native, who had two children, a son named Mark and a daughter whose name has not been released to the public. The newlyweds relocated to New York shortly after they tied the knot in the hopes that Applewhite could launch a career as a professional singer and actor, but unfortunately, upon being made to grapple with a streak of failed Broadway auditions, his ambitions of becoming a nationally renowned vocalist were quickly dashed. Disheartened and suddenly ambivalent about his life's purpose, he entered the Union Theological Seminary of Virginia in Richmond, where he planned to take a three-year course, the completion of which would grant him ordination in the Presbyterian Church. He took a few courses on theology, as well as the Old and New Testaments for two semesters, undoubtedly with the thought of resigning himself to simply carrying on his father's legacy, but he quickly realized that a life in the ministry, while noble, was not his calling. As such, he withdrew himself from the seminary and moved to the city of Gastonia in North Carolina with his wife.

In Gastonia, Applewhite decided to recalibrate his aspirations and gave his fervent passion for music and theater another whirl. With that, he accepted the posts of music director and assistant to the pastor at the local First Presbyterian Church, for which he received a reasonable salary. He thrived in this new environment, and much of his confidence was restored. He restructured and refined the church choir, and he was supposedly so successful in his endeavors that he helped to boost attendance at Sunday services. A patron of the First Presbyterian, Linda Starnes, harked back to Applewhite's brilliance and magnetism in an interview years later. He was, as Starnes described him, "drop-dead handsome...[and] when he got up to sing, looked and sounded like an angel." She added, "One thing I remembered about him all these years was his eyes and smile. I can see how he would have mesmerized people."

Applewhite also got along famously with his colleagues. He had an especially close friendship with Edith Warren, who played the organ for the church's children's choir. She, too, praised his mellifluous vocals and arresting stage presence, and she applauded his initiative and superior aptitude for leadership. Edith and her husband also went on regular double-dates with Applewhite and his wife during his two years with the church, which allowed her to see yet another side of him. He was an entertaining conversationalist with a great sense of humor, was comfortable in the kitchen, and had a taste for mutton.

By all accounts, Applewhite appeared to have been a family man. He was devoted to his children and always went out of his way to put a smile on their faces. "He once found a tree and put it in his Volkswagen Beetle," said Warren. "He put the tree in the living room of his house...painted it white and hung turquoise decorations on it. It wasn't a Christmas tree, just a fun tree for the kids when they were little."

Applewhite, like other eligible and able-bodied men his age, was conscripted into the army in 1954. He served as an instructor in the Army Signal Corps and was shuffled around during his two years of service in places such as the Austrian city of Salzburg by the German border, as well as White Sands, New Mexico. Fortunately, he was drafted several months after the conclusion of the Korean War, so he never participated in military combat. He was awarded the rank of Sergeant and honorably discharged in 1956.

Following his discharge, Applewhite continued to build his budding career in the domestic music industry. He performed in a few low-budget local musicals in Colorado and Texas, and he signed on as choir director in other churches such as the First Unitarian Church and St. Mark's Episcopal Church in Houston. He also secured the post of assistant music professor at the University of Alabama in 1959, where he remained for at least a year or two.

Applewhite forged an immediate bond with his students, who were drawn to the professor's ostensible humility and approachability in spite of his stupendous talent and expertise on the subject. For starters, he did not answer to "Mr. Applewhite," "Mr. Marshall," or any other formalities, insisting upon being addressed as simply "Herff." Said Neely Bruce, a former student of Applewhite's at the University of Alabama, "When Herff...came to the university...he didn't look at all like a professor. He was very casual, very laid-back. There was no hint that all this catastrophe was looming in his future...He had a lot of charisma...He would have the audience in the palm of his hand."

It was during this time that the 28-year-old Applewhite began to express a marked interest in aliens and extraterrestrial life. He penned a few essays about the mysteries of the cosmos, the infinite nature of the universe, and the existence of alien life forms on other planets, some of which he openly shared with his students. Be that as it may, his interest in these subjects, while spirited, still seemed to be contained in the sense that he never overtly pushed his unconventional beliefs on those around him.

Throughout the early 1960s, Applewhite also experimented with other professions outside of the music business, at one point enjoying a stint as an occupational therapist at a tuberculosis sanatorium just outside of Boulder, Colorado. He eventually returned to Houston, where he was employed as director of the music department at the private Basilian-run University of St. Thomas. At the same time, he graduated to the next stage of theatrical stardom, and was cast in 15 productions for the Houston Grand Opera, starring alongside the Spanish operatic icon Placido Domingo in *Faust* and *Carmen*. His performances were met with rave reviews. A critic for *Opera News*, who attended a showing of *Hansel and Gretel* in 1966, in which he played the role of "Father," praised Applewhite's "resonant, blessedly audible baritone." He also secured roles in performances staged by the Corpus Christi Symphony, the J.S. Bach Society, and the Houston Symphony.

Unfortunately, Applewhite's life began to fall apart towards the late 1960s. His marriage soured, and when he and his wife filed for divorce in 1968, the latter was granted full custody of their children. A little over two years later, he suffered nervous breakdowns and psychotic episodes, and he was subsequently dismissed from his post at St. Thomas. What triggered his mental health issues remains a matter of debate.

His former student, Bruce, shined a light on one of the rumors that swirled regarding his abrupt departure from the university. Applewhite had apparently been making moves to quit his day job and transition to a full-time resident performer at the Houston Grand Opera. Applewhite was in the midst of a rehearsal for his greatest role yet, the part of Olin Blitch in Carlisle Floyd's *Susannah*, when he became overwhelmed by the stress of it all and experienced an anxiety attack so severe that he was hospitalized. His father's untimely death in 1971 only exacerbated his problems.

Some surmised that he was merely undergoing an existential crisis, and that his depression had been brought on by the turbulent social and political climate of the United States, left in disarray by the Vietnam War, the Cold War, and other seemingly perennial nationwide crises. The most prominent theory, however, allegedly revolved around Applewhite's unspoken, but well-known struggle with his sexuality, which many believe was the primary cause of the demise of his marriage. It is believed that he was fired when his sexual relationship with a male graduate student was exposed. His Catholic employers, who wanted to distance themselves from the scandal and wrongful dismissal lawsuits, simply attributed the reasons for his sacking to "health problems of an emotional nature."

The involuntary outing and his unexpected expulsion from St. Thomas understandably left Applewhite bitter, confused, and inconsolable. Some say he had been let go from the University of Alabama for similar reasons, and perhaps not surprisingly, considering his strict Christian upbringing and the primitive social norms of the era, he was deeply conflicted and guilt-ridden about his sexual identity. On at least one occasion, he expressed to one of his partners his desire to one day become enlightened enough to enter a genuine, platonic relationship free of all romantic and sexual distractions, one that would last for a lifetime. It wasn't long after this that Applewhite claimed he began to hear voices.

Interestingly enough, when asked about these rumors in an interview conducted in March 1997, Father Patrick Braden, who served as the university president between 1967 and 1979, repudiated all of them. He claimed to have no knowledge of Applewhite's homosexuality and further insisted that Applewhite had never even been fired. According to Braden, Applewhite had tendered his resignation voluntarily to seek help for his degenerating mental health.

Whatever the reason, Applewhite's mental faculties became unquestionably compromised. His colleagues at the university, the opera house, and local theater groups alike noticed an alarming change in his behavior – gone was the quick-witted, articulate, and mild-tempered fellow they had come to love and respect, only to be replaced by a nervous, paranoid, and frazzled individual with a perpetually crazed look in his eyes. Things only worsened upon his return from a weekend trip to Galveston Beach, where he had supposedly been struck by a transformative vision extended to him by the Lord Himself. Hayes Parker, a close friend of Applewhite's, recalled, "He said a presence had given him all the knowledge of where the human race had come from and where it was going. It made you laugh to hear it, but Herff was serious." The mother of Patrick Swayze, Patsy, worked with Applewhite at a local theater production and echoed Hayes' sentiments in a separate interview: "[He had begun] to act strangely, talking about UFOs and preaching this strange religion." Patsy further noted that Applewhite frequently rambled on about mankind's ignorance to the true meaning of life, as well as the impending apocalypse.

Records reveal that Applewhite was admitted to Houston Hospital in the spring of 1972. According to his sister Louise, he had suffered from a near-fatal heart blockage, which she believed left him with lasting brain damage, thereby cementing his psychosis. Others say that he had checked himself into the psychiatric wing in the hopes of being "cured" of his homosexuality. Either way, most believe it was at this very hospital that he first became acquainted with a 44-year-old nurse by the name of Bonnie Lu Trusdale Nettles. This was confirmed by Applewhite himself years later, though he denied being hospitalized and claimed that he had met the nurse when he was visiting an ailing colleague. Conversely, Nettles' eldest daughter, Terrie, asserted that Applewhite was her older brother's vocal coach at a small theater company in Houston.

Regardless of how they first met, Nettles left an indelible impression on him, to say the least. Nettles, who was four years his senior, graduated from the Hermann Hospital School of Professional Nursing in Houston in 1948. Her devout Baptist upbringing notwithstanding, she developed an obsessive interest in a relatively modern pseudoscience known as "Theosophy," which was essentially a mix of astrology and the occult. Theosophists believed it was possible to make psychic contact with departed souls, and Nettles was inducted into the Houston Lodge of the Theosophical Society in February 1966. She conducted seances, calculated astrological charts, and performed divination readings – often unsolicited – for her family, friends, colleagues, and other believers. Her fixation on the paranormal did nothing to help her floundering marriage with Joseph Segal Nettles and increasingly strained relationship with her four children.

Her clairvoyance and soothsaying abilities, she claimed, were God-given gifts and were perfected through not only decades of practice, but also the guidance of "Brother Francis," the ghost of a monk who had died in Greece roughly two centuries ago. "He stands beside me when I interpret the charts," Nettles explained. "There can be several meanings to them, and if I'm wrong, he will correct me."

Nettles believed that she and Applewhite were destined to cross paths, and that it was literally written in the stars. Several years before, said Nettles, another seer foresaw that she would meet a tall and slender gentleman with fair skin and sandy-blond hair in the year 1972. Lo and behold, Applewhite fit the description to a tee, and unlike many others who would have bolted at the unironic mention of the supernatural, Applewhite was moved by Nettles' unapologetic authenticity and captivated by her bottomless knowledge in these subjects. He supposedly became so excited when she offered him a reading that he leapt up from his seat and raced to his car to fetch a copy of his birth certificate.

Nettles was astounded by the revelatory results of her readings. Applewhite, she declared, was a prophet handpicked by God, and he had been sent on a divine quest to lead his disorientated flock (mankind) away from the dark trail to perdition and back on the path to the Kingdom of Heaven. To be deemed worthy enough to carry out this sacred mission, Applewhite had to cleanse himself of all impurities, including his "unnatural" sexual urges, and liberate himself from all unnecessary burdens.

Given all that, some believe that Applewhite, who became the face of the cult, was an unwitting pawn who had been manipulated to do Nettles' bidding. However, it might be fair to argue that both were equally troubled, and they mutually enabled and fostered the delusions of each other. Indeed, Applewhite claimed that he began to see Brother Francis himself shortly thereafter.

Regardless of where they met, Applewhite and Nettles quickly became inseparable and wholly dependent on one another. Their intense bond, which became stronger with each passing day, far surpassed one of normal friendship, but their relationship reportedly remained completely platonic. The one-year anniversary of their first meeting and ensuing "union," so to speak, would coincide with the passing of the Comet Kohoutek, first sighted on March 7, 1973. Throughout the years, the dubious duo adopted a number of monikers, dubbing themselves "Bo and Peep" (a reference to their mission to round up aimless sheep), "Winnie and Pooh," "Tiddly and Wink," "Guinea and Pig," "Do and Ti," or simply, "The Two."

A 1974 picture of Comet Kohoutek

Odd fantasies aside, they completed one another in a sense. Eli Ewing, author of *Heaven's Gate Website: The Group is Gone, the Religion Lives On*, explained, "They each had strengths that they brought to the pairing – Applewhite with his dreams, visions, and out-of-body experiences, and Nettles with her explanations of dreams [and visions]." "I felt I had known her forever," Applewhite later said of his partner. This was a sentiment that Nettles requited, saying, "We have known each other in previous lives."

Both Louise and Applewhite's ex-wife Pearce exerted every effort to steer him away from Nettles, utilizing logic and scientific reasoning. When those failed, they cited Biblical passages that contradicted Nettles' ludicrous claims, but all the efforts were to no avail. Just weeks later, Applewhite severed all ties with his ex-wife, children, siblings, relatives, and friends, and he fully committed himself wholeheartedly to his heavenly quest.

He traveled to Dallas and knocked on Louise's door unannounced to deliver the worrying news. Naturally, Louise begged him to reconsider. "I said to him, 'What's the matter with you? That's not the real you,' His response was, 'You just don't know the real me.'"

Meanwhile, Nettles' husband divorced her, and she promptly lost custody of all her children.

The Mission

Applewhite and Nettles, who quit her nursing job without giving notice, pooled all their savings together and erected the Christian Art Center, a "metaphysical bookstore" within the First Unitarian Church in downtown Houston. Most days, Nettles manned the counter, peddling literature on religion, philosophy, art, and music, as well as the occult and other esoteric subjects. About a month later, the duo established a spiritual center known as the "Know Place," which provided intimate classes on Theosophy and other forms of mysticism. Applewhite supposedly moonlighted as a music director at the church to fund these ventures and to cover the couple's basic expenses.

Business was abysmal, and the proprietors of these enterprises hemorrhaged an increasing amount of cash every month. It was clear they were in need of a new plan, and to them, it made no sense to wait for their future disciples to stumble upon them on their own, particularly if they were to operate out of such an obscure location. Instead, to spread their gospel and build a following as quickly and as efficiently as possible, they had to step out of their comfort zones and deliver their message to the masses themselves. As such, on January 1, 1973, they shuttered the bookstore and spiritual center and dropped the keys into the landlord's mailbox.

The duo subsequently moved into a vacant room for rent at a small ranch house in the Texas Hill Country and locked themselves in their room for the next six weeks, only venturing out once a day to grab some food from the canteen. For hours on end, they meditated, consulted astrological charts, and channeled spirits through seances for guidance to purify their auras. They deliberately avoided alcohol, cigarettes, and sexual intercourse, so as to reboot the "programming" of their bodies, which they referred to as "vehicles." When they finally resurfaced from their self-assigned isolation, they donated all their material possessions and excess cash – barring a change of clothes or two, a single pair of shoes each, and an old sports car – to nearby shelters and charity organizations. After that, they purchased a medium-sized tent and some camping gear.

The cryptic couple next set off on their cross-country journey in mid-February of 1973. They lived like common vagrants, usually camping in parks overnight, and when they managed to score a motel room, they snuck out the rear entrance without footing the bill. They typically ate nothing but bread rolls, swiped food from grocery stores, only drank plain water, and dined and dashed regularly. They extenuated these acts of petty theft by chalking them up to a test from God, and they showed little remorse as they believed themselves to be exempt from human laws.

As Applewhite and Nettles flitted from one city to the next in search of followers, the pair visited local libraries, where they studied hagiographies centered on St. Francis of Assisi, among other saints, and memorized passages from the New Testament in their battered copy of the King

James Bible. They pored over books on Theosophy authored by the religion's co-founder, Helena Blavatsky, as well as literature on asceticism, Christology, existential philosophy, and other related schools of thought. Applewhite, ever the avid reader, also devoured science fiction novels, in particular the works of Arthur C. Clarke and Robert Heinlein. He also watched reruns of *Star Trek*, which debuted in 1966, religiously.

Blavatsky

In May 1974, the couple managed to persuade an old mutual friend from Houston, through a series of letters, to embrace their teachings. This woman would become their first recruit, and with that, their cult got its start.

Applewhite and Nettles happened upon yet another game-changing revelation two months later. The couple was camping by the Oregonian city of Gold Beach, leafing through the Book of Revelation, when it suddenly dawned on them that the telltale passage, found in Chapter 11, offered instructions: "And I will empower my two witnesses, and they will prophesy for 1,260 days, clothed in sackcloth. These witnesses are the two olive trees and the two lampstands that stand before the Lord...If anyone wants to harm them, fire proceeds from their mouths and devours their enemies. In this way, anyone who wants to harm them must be killed...When the two witnesses have finished their testimony, the beast that comes up from the Abyss will wage war with them, and will overpower and kill them...But after three and a half days, the breath of life from God entered the two witnesses, and they stood on their feet...And the witnesses heard a loud voice from Heaven saying, 'Come up here.' And they went up to heaven in a cloud as their enemies watched them...”

Applewhite and Nettles came to the conclusion that they were the two witnesses referenced in Revelation, and they became resolved to fulfill the Biblical prophecy, no matter the cost. The reinvigorated duo took pen to paper and composed a pamphlet in which they claimed that Christ had been reincarnated in Texas, his new vessel was Applewhite, and that Applewhite and Nettles had been chosen to carry out God's will as dictated in the Book of Revelation.

These were arguably among the least bizarre of their declarations. Applewhite in particular was an ardent proponent of the “ancient astronauts” or “ancient aliens” theory, which maintained that Martians visited Earth millions of years ago and populated the Earth with its first humans, and that these godly extraterrestrial life forms would one day return to the planet and retrieve only the worthiest of souls. Applewhite became convinced that God was, in fact, an almighty alien, and he surmised that the extraterrestrial spirit that once occupied Christ now resided in his “vehicle.” Furthermore, Applewhite and Nettles warned that doomsday was fast approaching, which they referred to as “The Demonstration.” On this day, they would lead the charge against the demonic beasts and hounds released from Hell, whom they named the “Luciferians.” Though they would emerge victorious, they, too, would perish, but they would be brought back to life, whereupon they would board a flying saucer and be whisked off to the Kingdom of God. They reiterated that only their most loyal, committed, and pure-hearted followers would be able to transcend alongside them to the “Next Level.”

Applewhite, Nettles, and their convert distributed these pamphlets at each one of their stops and spoke at local churches and spiritual workshops, during which they introduced themselves as “The Two” or “The UFO Two.” To their dismay, their ideas were poorly received at best, and their efforts were further thwarted by another pitfall on August 28, 1974 when Applewhite failed to pull over when flagged by state troopers in Harlingen, Texas and proceeded to lead the police on a high-speed chase. When Applewhite was eventually cornered, he was arrested for theft of a rental car. Nettles, in the passenger seat, was also apprehended after the cops found a number of stolen cards in her possession. She was charged with credit card fraud.

Their mugshots were a sight to behold. Applewhite appeared far older than his 43 years of age. He was gaunt, with wrinkled cheeks and disheveled hair that was generously streaked with grays and whites, a far cry from the attractive and well-groomed youngster he once was. Nettles' mugshot showed an overweight, drab-looking woman with crudely cropped hair. Like Applewhite, she was hardly recognizable compared to past photographs.

Applewhite in the 1970s

The charges against Nettles were quickly cleared, but Applewhite, on the other hand, was detained and later extradited to St. Louis. There, Applewhite refused to admit to any wrongdoing, and according to public defender Tim Braun, he contended that "a force from beyond the Earth made [him] keep [the stolen] car." Obviously, Applewhite's defense did nothing to help his case, and he was given a four-month or six-month sentence, which he served in the St. Louis county jail.

He made use of his time behind bars, continuing to research and flesh out their purpose and objectives in another essay. In the meantime, Nettles slipped back into her nurse scrubs, taking up a post at a small hospital in Houston. She quit her job upon Applewhite's release, used her earnings to purchase a used car and other camping essentials, and got back on the road.

It is only fair to note that the two had no intention of becoming persistent thieves and career squatters, and they apparently attempted to make an honest living to fund their divine quest on several occasions. At one point, they opened a delicatessen and sandwich shop called "Sunshine Company" in Taos, New Mexico, supposedly financed by a small bundle of insurance money they won from a car accident. They then crafted homemade crosses that they sold to a mom-and-pop Christian gift shop in Las Vegas. When their car broke down in Portland, Oregon some weeks later, they pawned off what little possessions they had to spare, took up a temporary job excavating septic tanks, and acquired another used car. After they were unable to find seasonal work, they panhandled, borrowed, accepted donations from magnanimous civilians, and sold blood and other bodily fluids wherever they could.

In time, the precariousness and laboriousness of their nomadic lifestyle began to take its toll on them. After some contemplation, The Two decided to renounce their usage of credit cards and rental cars, which they branded "tools of the Devil," and with the clock steadily ticking, they concluded that it was time to ramp up their gospel-spreading endeavors. Undeterred by their past stumbling blocks, they continued to produce more flyers, posters, and other advertisements for initiatory meetings, desperately hoping to expand their "crew." They originally christened themselves the "Anonymous Sexaholics Celibate Church," but they eventually took into account the negative feedback on their name, which many found to be unappealing and aggressive, and rebranded themselves the "Human Individual Metamorphosis." Only much later was their name shortened to "Heaven's Gate."

The reinvention of their image, as well as the refinement of their mission statement, paid off, as the attendance at these meetings began to soar. Prospective initiates learned that they were in the presence of hallowed, extraterrestrial representatives beamed down from Heaven, one of whom was the second coming of Christ, and that they had been instructed to amass a flock and escort them to the Next Level. They called their quest an "experiment" and jointly referred to themselves as "Guinea and Pig." Applewhite, the "lab instructor," did the bulk of the speaking, while Nettles chimed in intermittently with supplementary comments. The Two rarely conversed with the participants at length and only briefly acknowledged those who offered up their phone numbers, promising to reach out to them soon.

By March 1975, Applewhite, Nettles, and their first member had moved onto Ojai, located roughly 85 miles northwest of Los Angeles. In Ojai, they handed out copies of the wordy exposition Applewhite had written in his cell the previous year. An excerpt regarding Applewhite's thoughts on human metamorphosis and transcendence reads, "A member of the next kingdom finds favor with one who is willing to endure all of the necessary growing pains of weaning himself totally from his human condition...The idea that a good life leads to heaven is as silly as believing that if a caterpillar 'dies a good caterpillar, it will mysteriously awaken in a rose blossom and live there forever with the king butterfly.' People, like caterpillars, must go through a chrysalis stage, [discarding their old shells and] overcoming their humanness in preparation for life in the Next Level..."

It's unclear whether they believed these New Age metaphors and alternative, mystic words would be popular among Californians, but their message hit home with numerous residents in these parts. Two new recruits were added, a mother and her adult daughter, and the following month, a group of 80-100 people who learned of the meeting through the posters plastered all over town gathered at the spacious Hollywood Hills home of another potential convert named Joan Culpepper. The attendees were mesmerized by the simplicity of the oddly charming duo, clad in old sweatpants and muddy desert boots, and enthralled by the novelty and candidness of their pitch, which was peppered with *Star Trek* terminology. They were even more stunned when the extraterrestrial Christ incarnate claimed that his alien superiors had been communicating with him via the popular television show. "They laid it all out clearly," Culpepper later recalled. "They were tough. They said that they would die or be assassinated, and that those who decided to follow them would travel to a high level of existence with the help of a spaceship."

Interested parties were asked to fill out a questionnaire that would help determine whether they were ready for their exhaustive "personal transformation." The following are a few of the questions listed:

"1. Can you follow instructions without adding your own interpretation?

2. Can you deliver instructions as you receive them, or do they change according to your computer?

6. Do you put tasks off – procrastinate?

8. Do you use more of something than is adequate (e.g. excessively high cooking flame, more toothpaste than necessary, etc.)?

10. Are you sensitive when approaching another individual about something you want to discuss? Do you permit that individual the choice to continue what he is doing, or do you force him to drop it in order to give attention to you?"

Remarkably, 24 of the attendees agreed to meet Applewhite and Nettles in Gold Beach in a fortnight. Among these new recruits were Jacqueline Leonard, a beloved grandmother from Iowa who would become the oldest member of the cult, as well as a former model-turned-homemaker named Judith Rowland and an 18-year-old Air Force pilot trainee named Dick Joslyn. Other converts included a traveling salesman, a television producer, and a certified public accountant.

On May 5, 1975, the two dozen new recruits, who had sold off all their possessions and abandoned their homes during the past two weeks, assembled at their meeting place in Gold Beach as promised, ready to take on the quest for a higher level of existence and to fully immerse themselves in the teachings of Applewhite and Nettles. It was at this stage that the leaders asked to be addressed as "Bo and Peep," the divine shepherds of their growing flock. The "crew" joined Bo and Peep on their cross-country travels, touring other parts of Oregon before heading on to Medicine Bow, Wyoming, the Bonny Reservoir area in Colorado, and remote towns in Washington. They invited new recruits and locals unversed in their cause to attend their mobile "classrooms" for a better grasp of their cause.

In short order, Applewhite and Nettles were given a taste of internal dissension for the first time when Culpepper and a handful of other recruits began to take issue with the cult's puritanical rules and warped idea of discipline. Nettled by the constant barrage of questions and growingly caustic remarks, Applewhite and Nettles made the decision to remove Culpepper and other non-compliant members, leaving them stranded in Sedona, Arizona. Culpepper was livid at having been forsaken by these supposedly enlightened individuals, and she took it upon herself to track them down and show up at their recruitment meetings. She pressed them for answers for several months, racked with guilt at having roped her friends into what she now believed to be an extremely dangerous cult. As Culpepper put it, "The last time I saw them was about 1976 in Salt Lake City. When I walked in that night, the two of them just got up and left. They saw me as their Judas and thought that I was going to kill them."

Culpepper eventually halted the futile pursuit and took other steps to secure the closure that she sought. She went on to establish two halfway houses to help former cult members such as herself to get back on their feet. The first asylum, located in Los Angeles' Topanga Canyon, was dedicated to ex-members of Heaven's Gate, and the second, erected in San Francisco, aided runaways from the Peoples Temple.

Meanwhile, Applewhite and Nettles did not allow themselves to become discouraged by the mounting setbacks, and they kept their eyes firmly fixed on the prize. The roving cult forged on with their trek across the West Coast, and whenever funds were running low, they settled in remote countryside towns for several weeks. Some members acquired temporary positions as restaurant servers, store clerks, deliverymen, and other minimum-wage jobs. Some knocked on the doors of local churches and requested monetary donations. Others set up shop on street corners and relied on the kindness of strangers for food and gas money.

In the late summer of 1975, the crew set their sights on the famously liberal and "alternative" crowd in the Bay Area. They churned out more flyers, printed on bright red paper, and personally delivered notices to the offices of local publications. Many of these posters targeted Bay Area colleges, and one such poster addressing the students and faculty of the University of San Francisco bore the title "UFO's [sic] in San Francisco Area" in big, bolded letters with the following byline: "Why they are here; who they have come for; [and] when will they land." The body of the text contained a brief introduction of the agenda, as well as a misleading disclaimer:

> "Two individuals say they were sent from the level above human, and will return to that level in a spaceship (UFO) within the next [three] months. This man and woman will discuss how the transition from the human level to the next level is accomplished, and when this may be done.

> "This is not a religious or philosophical organization recruiting membership. However, the information has already prompted a number of individuals to devote their total energy to the transitional process. If you have ever entertained the idea that there might be a real PHYSICAL level in space beyond the Earth's confines, you will want to attend this meeting."

To the disappointment of those who responded to these flyers, The Two only made an appearance at the first meeting on the circuit, which was held at Cañada College in Redwood City on August 25. A number of gatherings were scheduled for the same day (the event advertised on the flyer above, for instance, was also set for August 25), and cult members representing The Two were tasked with speaking at the other assemblies, also held in the auditoriums of Stanford University, San Francisco State, and the Sunnyvale Civic Center. These meetings were a smash hit, attracting an average of 800 people each.

To be fair, many, if not most of those who showed did so expecting a laugh or to be entertained by some strange spectacle. There was, however, no pageantry involved - it was merely a seemingly run-of-the-mill forum, presented by two speakers seated behind a cheap plastic table. It would have been a rather dull event, too, had it not been for the subject matter at hand.

Those who expressed genuine interest in the subject matter were split into two camps. Some were turned off by the manner in which the speakers delivered their message, which they thought to be borderline belligerent. "The pitch is like that of a used-car salesman," remarked Peter Edler, who attended a meeting on the Tiburon campus of San Francisco State. "If you don't buy now, you'll never get a deal like this again...They [even] had enough nerve to tell me to leave my kids behind."

For others, particularly those who saw Applewhite in the flesh, it was a life-changing experience. His comportment, to start with, was inexplicably hypnotic. He was, as he claimed, a sapient, otherworldly being who possessed unimaginable powers and held the key to all of life's previously unanswerable questions. Some attendees, who soon became converts, insisted that all thoughts and mental images immediately vanished from their minds the moment he walked past them. One convert, who later withdrew himself from the cult, even went so far as to claim that he had an out-of-body episode when Applewhite laid a hand on his shoulder. According to him, he had momentarily been transported to the cockpit of a flying saucer, an experience so crystal-clear and palpable that he could feel one of the control levers in his grasp.

Another pivotal seminar led by Applewhite and Nettles took place on September 14. 200 interested parties congregated at the Fir Room of the Bayshore Inn in Waldport, Oregon, for which a "Mr. Simons" paid $50 for the hour. Like the fresh converts from the Bay Area colleges, the audience was bewitched by Applewhite's mysteriously entrancing demeanor. One attendee described the "strange, shiny look" of his glacial blue eyes, "almost as if they were sightless." She added, "His speech sounded as if it were being played on a machine and was turned on and off automatically...He didn't seem to blink his eyes at any time except to tip his head back at regular intervals and half-close both eyes. A robot was the only comparison I could make."

The audience listened with rapt attention as the duo urged those who fit the mold to consider this once-in-a-millennium opportunity. Some attendees later reported seeing a mystifying, flickering halo of light dancing around the speakers' heads, but a few were unnerved by what they described as a lingering "aura of death" hovering above them. Their discomfort only heightened when the orators informed them that they had been "marked for death" with the nonchalance of one recounting what they had for breakfast that morning, and that they were fully prepared to "return to the Next Level." The Demonstration and subsequent departure for their home planet, they announced, would unfold in a week's time.

Seven days later, dozens of people met on a windswept clifftop at the Colorado National Monument park, a large fraction of them familiar faces from Bayshore Inn. There, they waited patiently – hour after hour, then day after day – for a majestic, iridescent spaceship to descend from the open sky. Needless to say, a celestial spacecraft never arrived, but even as the crowd did begin to thin out at various points, The Two miraculously managed to recruit another 20-30 people. A member who identified himself only as "Sawyer" claimed there were as many as 34 who remained. The new recruits, as per the cult's laws, relinquished their homes and possessions, ditched their jobs (many of them high-paid, prestigious posts), and abruptly bade farewell to their loved ones, completely jettisoning their former lives for their new family.

The tremendous turnouts at Bayshore and past venues had attracted no media coverage, but the news that over 20 Waldeport locals simply left without warning generated a whirlwind of negative publicity. Along with local media, national TV programs such as *CBS Evening News* and publications like *Newsweek* and the *New York Times* covered the incident. Confused journalists wondered why normal people, some of whom had wealth, would forsake their lives for such an absurd cause. Robert Rubin, for example, reportedly signed away four houses, a farmhouse, and seven plots of land measuring 10 acres total. Applewhite and Nettles were depicted in an unflattering light, with some speculating that brainwashing and pressure tactics were at play. Weeks later, however, other publications challenged the authors of these sensational articles, accusing them of blowing things out of proportion and eliciting hysteria just to plump up sales.

On Halloween, over 100 crew members and potential converts from at least 23 states – this time along with a smattering of reporters – convened once again at Tilden Park in Berkeley. The congregation proceeded over to the marshy ground alongside Lake Anza, where they were greeted by a Heaven's Gate representative. He revealed that The Two, sadly, were unable to grace them with their presence, as they were "preparing to be assassinated or killed" within the next couple of weeks. He encouraged the attendees to take a cue from the leaders and provided them with instructions on how to best reprogram their vehicles. According to Mark Trautwein of the *Berkeley Gazette*, multiple crew members were certain that they could sense the "chemical changes" rippling throughout their mortal shells, which would "render them unrecognizable when aboard the spaceship."

No such spaceship ever came, but the string of false prophecies that followed, one of which was set for the eruption of Mount St. Helens in 1980, did nothing to shatter the faith that the majority of the members had in The Two. In fact, the cult continued to grow, and members respected the duo's transparency. Applewhite and Nettles always extended heartfelt apologies for miscalculating the date of The Demonstration, and they reminded their followers that they were free to leave at any time. When Joslyn chose to part ways with the group 15 years after his induction, Applewhite personally thanked Joslyn for his years of service, reassured him that there would be no hard feelings, and even paid for his bus ticket to Florida, a gesture that deeply moved him.

A Day in the Life

By the time *UFO Missionaries Extraordinary,* a comprehensive account of Heaven's Gate and the cult's leaders written by Brad Steiger and Hayden C. Hewes, hit the shelves in early 1976 and propelled the cult's fame to even greater heights, the crew already consisted of over 200 international members. However, rather than capitalize on their celebrity, Nettles proclaimed at a meeting in Kansas on April 21 that the "Harvest" had officially come to a close, meaning that they were no longer accepting new recruits. The next year, core membership dropped to roughly 70, and in the years that followed, it dropped under 50.

Applewhite and Nettles, who now went by "Do" and "Ti," appeared to have been unfazed by the substantial drop in their numbers. In their opinion, God was doing them a favor by weeding out the undeserving frauds and weakest links from the group. Life was indeed often grueling for those who remained, but they dutifully kept the faith, for they believed in the deepest depths of their hearts that the payoff would be worth it.

All in all, members ranged from their 20s to 70s and mostly hailed from states with the most UFO sightings per capita, specifically New Mexico, Texas, and Colorado. Many were once promising, productive members of the community until a traumatic event sent their lives into a tailspin. One of them was Julie LaMontagne, a former nursing student who graduated magna cum laude from the University of Massachusettes in 1974 before losing her best friend in a drowning accident and her father Jules to cancer in the same year. Similarly, Margaret Field, a talented public speaker and majorette, was crowned valedictorian of Las Plumas High School in 1969. She was a wildly popular student, and her peers once predicted that she would be governor or even president. She went on to graduate from Berkeley and was awarded a master's degree in computer science from UCLA, but her short-lived marriage left her in emotional dispair.

There were some whose initiation into the cult left their loved ones utterly dumbfounded. Michael Barr Sandoe, the extroverted but urbane son of an evangelical pastor, was affectionately remembered as the class clown and ambitious senior class president, and prior to joining the cult, he received numerous accolades for his service as a Desert Storm infantry paratrooper. The Minnesota-born Joyce Skalla, an ex-beauty queen, was married to a high-ranking Navy officer and a mother to two gorgeous twin daughters. She returned to school in Tulsa, Oklahoma, acquired a journalism degree, and served as coordinator for Byrd Community School before transitioning into a local TV personality. Skalla gave all of that up less than 48 hours after attending a Heaven's Gate meeting.

John Craig, an affluent businessman whose multiple properties included one of the largest dude ranches in all of Colorado, appeared to have been happily married and was a doting father of six. When his wife and kids returned from a swim meet held two towns over one July evening in 1975, they were horrified to discover that the patriarch – who had brought with him only a spare set of clothes, a small wad of cash, and his Chevy – was long gone. All he left behind was an emotionless note containing instructions on how to access his personal and business bank accounts.

Ladonna Brugato, whose sole quirk was the altar of crystals and candles next to her bed, was yet another who seemingly disappeared out-of-the-blue in 1994. Her landlord, Al Wallace, noted, "If you met her on the street, she would have been the girl-next-door who was simply trying to get by as a single mom. You never would have imagined that it could have gone this far..."

In the late 1970s, the cult began to take longer breaks from their itinerant lifestyle and settled down in various places for longer stretches of time. The cult was mainly funded by the $300,000 inheritance bequeathed to two of the crew members following the death of their family members, which they used to rent a few houses at a time, first in Denver, and later in Dallas-Fort Worth. Nearby residents gossiped about the peculiar behavior of the new tenants, who preferred to remain indoors behind closed curtains. From the outside looking in, it is difficult to imagine why anyone would willingly choose to live under such austere conditions. The fact that these followers chose to stay and willingly entertained their leaders' every whim was a true testament of their undying faith in The Two, as well as the power that they wielded over their disciples.

As noted above, members were made to surrender all their worldly possessions and strip themselves of their former identities completely, which at that time meant putting some parentless children up for adoption. They were to cease all communication with their family members and friends, effective immediately, excluding the occasional vaguely worded postcard. They were expected to forgo jewelry, facial hair, and other forms of personal expression, instead adopting near-identical buzzed and closely cropped hairstyles. To strengthen this illusion of "unity" further, each member was forced to renounce their human names and were assigned new appellations upon their arrival. All new names were six letters long and capitalized, consisting of a random collection of three letters followed by the suffix "ODY."

The cult adopted a strict dress code featuring dull, gender-neutral clothing in monochromatic colors. In the early days, members styled themselves in baggy, plain black clothes from head to toe, and they later began to don shapeless, gray, collarless tops so as to "emphasize modesty, comfort, and utilitarian value." More significantly, their fashion sense emulated the clothing style worn by the "Gray." the alien species that they would evolve into once they shed their mortal shells. Artistic renderings of a "Gray" alien – a bald, gray-skinned, androgynous life form with an oversized dome and giant, glassy black eyes, sporting a skintight silver spacesuit – were tacked onto the walls of these otherwise colorless and sparsely-furnished rental homes, representing the only decorations allowed on the premises.

This was unlike any stereotypical New Age cult, which usually championed free love and openly endorsed carnal relations, polyamory, alcohol, and drugs. Sexual intercourse, boozing, smoking, and anything else deemed a poisonous act or crutch – which, to the cult, included all negative emotions and thoughts – were prohibited. Corporeal desires and unhealthy vices, The Two reasoned, would only distract them from their mission. Some believed that the forced celibacy was a product of Applewhite's suppressed homosexuality. Others believe that the cult simply intended to live their lives as dictated by the anatomy and bodily functions of extraterrestrials. A common belief found in many UFO circles suggested that aliens were born without vocal chords and sexual organs, and therefore would have no sex drive.

On a related note, a partner was appointed for every member, supposedly according to whoever the member would find the least attractive. In a later interview, former member Leslie Light remembered her horror when a "crazy street person" had been assigned to her. These pairs were practically joined at the hip for 24 hours a day and were tasked with monitoring the other's behavior and activities. Members rotated partners approximately every six weeks as an extra precaution so as to keep the possibility of developing romantic feelings or excessively affectionate (even if platonic) feelings for one's partner at a minimum.

Applewhite was so zealous about his commitment to asceticism that he not only banned the act of hugging but even had himself surgically castrated. At least seven other members followed suit, doing so of their own volition. Initially, they tried to perform these operations in-house, and perhaps not surprisingly, their first attempt on Steven McCarter, now known as "SRRODY," resulted in a trip to the emergency room. Another member was allegedly instructed to toss SRRODY's testicles into the water of a nearby pier to eliminate the evidence. Due to this disastrous first attempt, later castrations were performed by former doctors and nurses in sketchy warehouses and other remotely located non-medical facilities.

The Two apparently justified this self-mutilation by citing Matthew 19:12, which reads, "There are eunuchs who are born so from their mother's womb; and there are eunuchs who are made so by men; and there are eunuchs who have made themselves so for the sake of the kingdom of heaven. Let him accept it who can." Another former member explained the cult's rationale further in an email sent to *Vice*: "As far as emotional human trappings, it was a difficult experience to shed all those things that are hard-wired into the flesh and blood, and also nurtured by human methods of raising children. It takes constant alert to not allow automatic reactions and habits to play out."

In addition to extensively detailed, tightly-packed timetables for daily chores and tasks, designed as such to keep their impure thoughts and natural urges at arm's length, The Two also drew up comprehensive dietary schedules for themselves, as well as the crew. Their eating habits were exceptionally clean, actively avoiding all sugary drinks excluding fruit juices, as well as fried foodstuffs. Their diets were rich with multivitamins. Plainly put, they found no enjoyment in their cuisine and only ate to sustain themselves and to minimize the pollutants within their vehicles.

Sometimes, the manner in which they consumed their food was unhealthy. Members, for instance, often underwent week-long juice cleanses, but mostly, as one member recounted, they believed that "moderation in small amounts of meat, chicken, and lots of vegetables and grains was key," as it "provided a balance that could supply [them] with the energy to work at our regular jobs while supplying the mental alertness to keep our focus and direction."

A treatise published by Applewhite, *Transfiguration Diet*, featured the dietary schedules and recipes the crew utilized, along with a collection of rough hand-drawn drawings of aliens in the kitchen. The Sunday timetable was as follows: "For breakfast, members were given a choice of wheat berries (honey and raisins) or an assorted fruit bowl. For lunch, served at 12:30, they tucked into a raw salad medley composed of lettuce, spinach, cucumber, broccoli, sprouts, carrots, and peas drizzled with olive oil, garlic, or vinegar dressing. At 14:30 sharp, members chugged four ounces of grape juice diluted in equal part water. Precisely an hour later, they snacked on two pears. At 17:10, the crew ingested six ounces of water mixed with a teaspoon of Cayenne. This was chased down by another teaspoon of wheat germ oil 10 minutes later. Then, at 17:30, they were served potato soup with a lettuce-and-spinach salad on the side, along with steamed corn, broccoli with a lemon wedge, and a baked potato garnished with green pepper, beets, and green beans. At 19:30, they swallowed a single red clover capsule, followed by a tablespoon of Molasses at 20:30, and three more capsules of Naturalax II at 21:30."

To their credit, The Two were a lot of things, but they weren't hypocrites. They adhered to an even stricter dietary schedule, timed to the minute. The following is a glimpse into Nettles' distinctive schedule, as shared by one of the members: "At 5:57PM, Nettles bathed. 24 minutes later, she took a vitamin pill, one of 32 consumed every 24 hours. At 6:36, she drank a liquid protein formula, and one hour later, she ate a cinnamon roll. At 9:54, she was back in bed for another two hours."

Entertainment was also rigorously regulated. Members were forbidden from reading unapproved books, newspapers, and other publications, and they were not to tune into radio and television news broadcasts, so as to keep them in the dark on current affairs. Only television programs selected by Applewhite, primarily *Star Trek, Star Wars, X-Files,* and *Close Encounters of the Third Kind*, were screened on the communal 72-inch TV. As fate would have it, Thomas

Nichols, one of The Two's most faithful followers, was the brother of actress Nichelle Nichols, who played Lieutenant Nyota Uhura in the original *Star Trek* series and movies.

The inordinate stringency and specificity of The Two's rules were not without their purposes, as they progressively pushed the boundaries of the members' obedience and loyalty. On movie nights, for starters, members were made to arrange themselves according to a seating chart. No one could leave the premises without their partners, with the exception of those who held jobs, and even they were required to sign out from a logbook each time, during which they would be given their license and car keys. Moreover, they were expected to undergo severe meditative periods The Two called "tomb time," during which members were prohibited from speaking, even to their partners, for several days at a time. Partners also tapped tuning forks on one another's heads for hours on end, so as to declutter their minds. Those who could not cut it were ejected from the cult immediately, and at one point, as many as 19 members were collectively expelled as a result.

Occasionally, Applewhite and Nettles saddled members with impromptu tasks that were as onerous as they were pointless, supposedly to test their fidelity to the cause. When the cult was stationed in Texas, The Two ordered all their members to stand outside under the open sky overnight, leaving them exposed to the elements – during which they were instructed to remain upright at all times – to welcome an incoming spaceship, which they believed to be the real deal. The group was finally summoned back to the house the following afternoon and congratulated for completing "the drill."

Under these punishing circumstances, members became totally reliant on their leaders and incessantly sought their approval. The Two were fully aware of the psychological hold they had on their disciples and employed other manipulation tactics to further solidify this codependency. *People* magazine contributor Laura Barcella explained, "[One time, Applewhite] and Nettles...called a meeting, which several members failed to attend. Rather than browbeat their recalcitrant underlings, The Two announced, sadly, that they were going to leave the group for a time to meditate on why they had failed in their leadership. When they returned hours later, members wept with shame and relief."

The oppressive rigidity of these routines began to slacken in later years. As emotionless as Applewhite and Nettles strove to be, they often exhibited flashes of human compassion, and even in the early days, they were known to make allowances for special cases. Grandma Leonard, for one, was permitted to correspond with her family on a regular basis, and in 1982, this "privilege" was extended to the other cult members, who were now entitled to short telephone calls with former loved ones. The following year, members who so wished were granted permission to reunite with family members for Mother's Day, under the condition that their trip be restricted to two days. They were also made to parrot the same cover story, in which they claimed that they had entered a distant monastery and were studying computers, hence their odd haircuts and clothes. This was, by most accounts, a believable alibi since many members had certified backgrounds in computer science and engineering, and as brief and rare as these short trips, phone calls, and letters back home were, they helped to alleviate the concerns of their families.

The cult reached a turning point on June 19, 1985, when Nettles, whose eye had been removed due to complications from liver cancer two years prior, succumbed to her illness. As might be expected, Nettles' death devastated Applewhite, who was unable to process her death and suffered even greater levels of psychosis. The core group, whose numbers had dwindled to 39, were equally floored by Ti's demise. "We were all devastated, most of all Do," said ex-member Frank Lyford, also known as ANDODY. "How could this happen?...We were all supposed to graduate together." All members except for one remained by Applewhite's side and made every effort to lift his spirits and redirect him back to their cause.

Applewhite eventually regained his composure, at least to some extent, but due to Nettles' untimely departure, the ideology that they had worked so hard to craft was falling apart at the seams. He returned to the drawing board and unveiled the crucial adjustments he made to their philosophy weeks later. Do, he announced, had no choice but to ascend to the Next Level, as she had been bursting with "too much energy to remain on Earth." She had already reached the pinnacle of enlightenment, Applewhite continued, and thus, their alien overlords decided to expedite her homecoming. On the other hand, he lagged several stages behind, and as such, his time had not yet come. Do was now eagerly waiting for their reunion, which was why they were in need of a proper plan that would ensure their simultaneous graduation, as they had originally intended. As a symbol of his imperishable commitment to his disciples, Applewhite purchased 39 gold bands, priced at $100 apiece, and wedded each one of them in a private ceremony.

The Departure

Heaven's Gate retreated into the shadows of obscurity towards the end of the 1980s and remained in such a dormant state for years that many on the outside erroneously assumed that they had gone extinct. The cult only reemerged from their seeming retirement in 1992, during which they renamed themselves "Total Overcomers Anonymous" and debuted a video series of their creation entitled *Beyond Human – The Last Call.* The segments had been filmed the previous year, and they essentially served as a longer, glorified introductory and recruitment video. On May 27, 1993, *USA Today* printed an advertisement sent in by cult members under the headline "UFO Cult Resurfaces with Final Offer." The day of reckoning, they warned, was upon them, and the entire human civilization would soon be "recycled."

Given how they lived, it is shocking that the cult's members were technological pioneers in the sense that Heaven's Gate was one of the first organizations to utilize the Internet to spread their message around the globe. The Heaven's Gate official website was developed under the cult's own accredited company, the aptly named "Higher Source Contract Enterprises." The team consisted of trained tech specialists who designed and coded websites, as well as produced original digital graphics for companies in various languages. A former member claimed, "Chances are your cellular phone or pager company [used] programs designed by our team of professionals. So do many banks and other major corporations." Their earnings were substantial enough that other members who previously had full-time jobs no longer needed the employment.

The cult marketed their web development and graphic design services under "The Difference" tab on their website. It read, "The individuals at the core of our group have worked closely together for over 20 years. During these years, each of us have developed a high degree of skill and know-how through personal discipline and concerted effort...[You can trust us to] provide advanced solutions at highly competitive rates." In January 1994, the group embarked on one last cross-country recruitment tour, stopping at 63 cities and towns across 22 states, which concluded in Boston.

The fateful sign Applewhite had so urgently yearned for came a year and a half later. This sign came in the form of the Comet Hale-Bopp, which was discovered by a pair of amateur astronomers named Alan Hale and Thomas Bopp on July 23, 1995. The passing of the comet was truly an unparalleled, glorious affair for the ages, as its last appearance dated back to over 4,200 years ago, when many of the ancient Egyptian pyramids were still new. The comet, which would remain visible in the Northern Hemisphere for 18 months straight between 1996 and 1997, surpassed the streak of the Great Comet of 1811.

Anxious to join Nettles on the Next Level, in October 1996, Applewhite and his 38 disciples (21 women and 17 men) secured a lease for a sprawling three-story, seven-bedroom, Mediterranean-style hilltop mansion measuring 9,200 square feet in Rancho Santa Fe, California, which would set them back a staggering $7,000 each month. On November 15, another vital element of the grand plan, their date of departure, took shape when Applewhite learned that an amateur photographer had captured a cryptic entity – an actual unidentified flying object – tagging along behind the comet. This mysterious object, Applewhite concluded, had to be the heaven-sent spaceship that they had prophesied, and it was coming to collect their souls.

The crew spent the following months meticulously preparing for their final exit, which was scheduled for the week that the comet was due to be closest to Earth. They purchased massive quantities of powdered barbiturates from Mexico, as well as 39 pairs of Nike '93 Decades, a plain black-and-white sneaker from the budget line, their only significance being its cheap $10 price tag. They also commissioned a fresh set of identical, specially designed uniforms: sleek, all-black collared jumpsuits, which they would wear on their literal self-made deathbeds. Triangular patches embroidered with the words "Heaven's Gate Away Team," set against a backdrop of shooting stars and a radiant sun burst, were sewn to each sleeve, a deliberate reference to Captain Kirk's exploration team. The week prior to the departure, the team recorded their farewell videos, and Applewhite's manifesto was videotaped separately.

At around 2:00 p.m. on March 21, 1997, the crew's last day on Earth, Applewhite and his 38 disciples filed into the Carlsbad branch of the Marie Callender's restaurant chain, where the group would have their celebratory last supper. Everyone in the party ordered the same meal – a large turkey pot pie, which they enjoyed with a blueberry cheesecake and an iced tea – which was noticeably more indulgent than the cult's traditional diet. Later that evening, the Heaven's Gate website was updated with an animated, flashing "Red Alert" graphic, along with the following message: "Hale-Bopp brings closure to Heaven's Gate...[The comet's] arrival is joyously very significant to us at 'Heaven's Gate.' The joy is that our Older Member in the Evolutionary Level Above Human...has made it clear to us that Hale-Bopp's approach is the 'marker' we've been waiting for – the time for the arrival of the spacecraft from the Level Above Human to take us home to 'Their World' – in the literal Heavens. Our 22 years of classroom here on planet Earth is finally coming to conclusion – 'graduation' from the Human Evolutionary Level. We are happily prepared to leave 'this world' and go with Ti's crew."

Over the next three days, members of the cult took turns laying themselves to eternal sleep, with 15 killing themselves the first day, another 15 the next day, and the remaining nine on the third day. Those scheduled to depart on the first shift consumed either vodka, pudding, or applesauce laced with lethal doses of phenobarbital and hydrocodone (the latter an opioid typically used for pain management), inserted their heads in tightly sealed plastic bags, and reclined themselves on their assigned beds. Those due to make their exit on the second day would then tidy up after their departed comrades before repeating the process. Applewhite, the last man standing, made one final sweep across the mansion, checking the pulses of his disciples to ensure that their souls had fully exited their vehicles. Only then did he lay himself to rest in the master bedroom.

A nominal member of the cult, Rio DiAngelo, hastened over to the mansion on March 26 as instructed by the letter he received in the mail that morning, and he reported the heartbreaking incident to the relevant authorities. The lifeless bodies of the cult members, which had entered the first stages of decomposition, were found laid out on their adjacent bunk beds. Squares of cloth in varying shades of violet were draped over their heads and upper torsos, so that only their black pants and Nike Decades were visible. Precisely $5.75 in identical bills and coins were found in each one of their pockets.

One might presume that their deaths, while pitiful and acutely distressing, were relatively peaceful, but the blood spatters on the walls and the pools of urine that stained the carpets suggest otherwise. A number of seemingly unused shotguns, rifles, and other assault weapons were apparently located in two sheds within the compound shortly afterwards. Given that there were no survivors, there was no way to determine the exact chain of events that took place in the residence.

In the wake of the mass suicide, it did not take long for America and the rest of the world to make a mockery out of Heaven's Gate members. *Saturday Night Live* aired a segment wherein a Nike symbol and the company's famous slogan, "Just do it," was superimposed onto actual photographs of the dead cult members just two weeks after the event. Even to this day, it is not uncommon to see "edgy" youths in homemade Heaven's Gate costumes for Halloween. All of that obscured the actual human cost of the event, and that the cult's members still deserve some common decency:

Dana Tracey Abreo, 35

Marshall Herff Applewhite, 66

Robert John Arancio, 46

Raymond Alan Bowers, 46

Ladonna Ann Brugato, 40

Margaret June Bull, 53

Cheryl Elaine Butcher, 42

Michael Howard Carrier, 48

Suzanne Sylvia Cooke, 54

Wayne "Nick" Cooke, 54

John M. Craig, 63

Betty Eldrie Deal, 64

Erika Ernst, 40

Alphonzo Foster, 44

Charles Humphrey, 56

Darwin Lee Johnson, 42

Jacqueline Opal Leonard, 72

Jeffrey Howard Lewis, 41

Gail Renee Maeder, 28

Steven Terry McCarter, 41

Joel Peter McCormick, 29

Yvonne McCurdy-Hill, 39

Julie LaMontagne, 45

David Geoffrey Moore, 41

Nancy Dianne Nelson, 45

Norma Jeane Nelson, 59

Thomas Alva Nichols, 59

Susan Elizabeth Nora Paup, 54

Lindley Ayerhart Pease, 41

Lucy Eva Pesho, 63

Margaret Ella Richter, 46

Judith Rowland, 50

Michael Barr Sandoe, 25

Brian Alan Schaaf, 40

Joyce Angela Skalla, 58

Gary Jordan St. Louis, 44

Susan Frances Strom, 44

Denise June Thurman, 44

David Cabot van Sinderen 48

Gordon Welch, 50

Sadly, the mass suicide was not the end of the horrific and tragic tale. 54-year-old Wayne Cook, the husband of the one of the deceased members, Suzanne Cooke, was despondent over his failure to join the crew in their final exit. On May 7, his corpse was found at the Holiday Inn Express on Leucadia Boulevard in Encinitas, about five miles away from the Rancho Santa Fe mansion. Cooke's companion, 56-year-old Charles Humphrey, who was laying alongside him, was found with a faint pulse and was subsequently revived at Scripps Memorial Hospital. The pair had attempted to mimic the crew's suicide methods, which had been publicized by the media, down to the last detail. They, too, were dressed in black slacks and Nike Decades, ingested a cocktail of vodka and barbiturates, and were each found with a $5 bill and three quarters in their pockets.

In a Heaven's Gate documentary produced by *History TV* that aired a few months later, Humphrey ruefully reflected on the crew's mass departure and made no mention of his unsuccessful suicide attempt. "I was so happy to hear that they were finally off this planet," said Humphrey. "I just wish that I was with them at that moment." Humphrey's dead body was discovered in a tent in the Arizona desert on February 21, 1998. He had slipped a plastic bag over his head and stuffed it with pipes connected to his car's exhaust pipe, as well as a tank labeled "carbon dioxide."

On November 22, 1999, the cult members' uniforms, shoes, and other personal effects were put up for bidding at a local auction. Profits generated by the curator of Los Angeles' Museum of Death and collectors of morbid memorabilia amounted to $32,707, part of which was used to cover the auction's costs. The rest was divvied up among the deceased's surviving family members. Nike immediately discontinued production of the '93 Decades for obvious reasons, but demand for that particular line of shoes skyrocketed, and they are now regarded as rare, limited-edition collector items. Today, buyers can typically find a pair of '93 Nike Decades listed on *eBay* at a starting bid of $6,660. The Rancho Santa Fe mansion, now referred to as the "Hale-Bopp House," still remains on the market, but its value dropped precipitously, going from its original $1.6 million to $668,000.

Incredibly, the cult, while a mere whisper of what it was in its heyday, still exists. Its official website is still in operation, supposedly run by a surviving member who calls himself "Telah," and it bears the exact same design – a chilling time capsule featuring outdated graphics, animations, and a fixed, pixelated background of twinkling stars, with a link to purchase a hard copy of their book. Other members, in addition to responding to emails, have taken to keeping the cause alive via more modern forms of social media. One member, Sawyer, currently runs a blog entitled "Sawyer Stands for Ti & Do's Heaven's Gate" and actively posts on and livestreams from his Twitter account under the handle "SawyerDoTi."

Online Resources

Other 20th century history titles by Charles River Editors

Other titles about Heaven's Gate on Amazon

Bibliography

Achenbach, J., & Fisher, M. (1997, March 30). THE CULT THAT LEFT AS IT LIVED. Retrieved December 25, 2020, from https://www.washingtonpost.com/archive/politics/1997/03/30/the-cult-that-left-as-it-lived/1e9baadb-f465-4a7a-8026-0ab7e4822139/

Arrillaga, P. (1997, March 30). Cult leader's son apologizes for father's actions. Retrieved December 25, 2020, from https://apnews.com/article/4b33621b0db2171404d5524c3fde0d64

Baig, E. C. (2019, July 2). UFOs: Where your state ranks for unexplained sightings. Retrieved December 25, 2020, from https://www.usatoday.com/story/tech/talkingtech/2019/07/02/states-with-most-ufo-sightings/1586103001/

Barcella, L. (2020, March 26). Heaven's Gate, 23 Years Later: Remembering 38 People Who Died with Cult Leader. Retrieved December 25, 2020, from https://people.com/crime/heavens-gate-22-years-later-remembering-lives-lost/

Bearak, B. (1997, April 28). Eyes on Glory: Pied Pipers of Heaven's Gate. Retrieved December 25, 2020, from https://www.nytimes.com/1997/04/28/us/eyes-on-glory-pied-pipers-of-heaven-s-gate.html

Borden, J. (2020, December 8). The Heaven's Gate Cult Was As American as Apple Pie. Retrieved December 25, 2020, from https://www.vanityfair.com/hollywood/2020/12/heavens-gate-cult-of-cults-docuseries-hbo-max

Breitman, D. (2019, April 1). Today in science: Comet Hale-Bopp. Retrieved December 25, 2020, from https://earthsky.org/space/this-date-in-science-comet-hale-bopp

Brock, M. (2020, December 17). The Legacy of Heaven's Gate. Retrieved December 25, 2020, from https://newportnewstimes.com/article/the-legacy-of-heavens-gate

Brooke, J. (1997, April 1). For Ex-Wife of Leader, No Wish for the Limelight. Retrieved December 25, 2020, from https://www.nytimes.com/1997/04/01/us/for-ex-wife-of-leader-no-wish-for-the-limelight.html?auth=login-google

Caffier, J. (2017, March 16). The Heaven's Gate Nikes and the Sneakerheads Who Collect Them. Retrieved December 25, 2020, from https://www.vice.com/en/article/kbynmn/the-heavens-gate-nikes-and-the-sneakerheads-who-collect-them

Cole, R. (2016). 10 Failed Doomsday Predictions. Retrieved December 25, 2020, from https://www.britannica.com/list/10-failed-doomsday-predictions

Colurso, M. (2020, December 13). 7 creepy things we learned about cult leader and former UA teacher Marshall Applewhite. Retrieved December 25, 2020, from https://www.al.com/life/2020/12/7-creepy-things-we-learned-about-cult-leader-and-former-ua-teacher-marshall-applewhite.html

Covarrubias, A. (1997, March 30). Relatives of Heaven's Gate cult seem resigned. Retrieved December 25, 2020, from https://www.southcoasttoday.com/article/19970330/news/303309960

Delloye, T. (2020, December 20). Madness of Heaven's Gate cult: HBO doc reveals how two Star Trek-obsessed Texans persuaded 39 cult members to 'exit their human vessels' in largest mass suicide in US history - and each with $5.75 in their pocket and wearing same Nike sneakers. Retrieved December 25, 2020, from https://www.dailymail.co.uk/news/article-9012075/Heavens-Gate-UFOs-cults-largest-mass-suicide-event-American-soil.html

Dowd, K. (2020, December 17). 'UFO Takes Man's Wife': When the Heaven's Gate cult recruited in the Bay Area. Retrieved December 25, 2020, from https://www.sfgate.com/sfhistory/article/hbo-max-heavens-gate-show-bay-area-15803962.php

Editors, A. I. (2013, January 2). Heaven's Gate — A timeline. Retrieved December 25, 2020, from https://www.apologeticsindex.org/498-heavens-gate-timeline

Editors, A. O. (2020). Heaven's Gate Suicide House. Retrieved December 25, 2020, from https://www.atlasobscura.com/places/hale-bopp-house

Editors, A. P. (1997, March 30). Authorities List Names of Suicide Victims. Retrieved December 25, 2020, from https://movies2.nytimes.com/library/national/0330suicide-list.html

Editors, B. C. (2020, July 17). Marshall Applewhite Biography. Retrieved December 25, 2020, from https://www.biography.com/crime-figure/marshall-herff-applewhite

Editors, C. B. (1998, February 20). 'Do Not Revive'. Retrieved December 25, 2020, from https://www.cbsnews.com/news/do-not-revive/

Editors, C. I. (2019). HEAVEN'S GATE CULT. Retrieved December 25, 2020, from https://www.crimeandinvestigation.co.uk/crime-files/heaven-s-gate-cult

Editors, C. N. (2011, April 6). Notorious Doomsday Prophets and Cults. Retrieved December 25, 2020, from https://www.cnbc.com/2011/04/06/Notorious-Doomsday-Prophets-and-Cults.html

Editors, C. T. (1997, March 30). ALIENATION FROM FAMILIES A COMMON PATH FOR VICTIMS. Retrieved December 25, 2020, from https://www.chicagotribune.com/news/ct-xpm-1997-03-30-9703300383-story.html

Editors, E. C. (2020, November 18). Applewhite, Jr., Marshall Herff (1931-1997). Retrieved December 25, 2020, from https://www.encyclopedia.com/science/encyclopedias-almanacs-transcripts-and-maps/applewhite-jr-marshall-herff-1931-1997

Editors, H. C. (2020, March 23). Heaven's Gate cult members found dead. Retrieved December 25, 2020, from https://www.history.com/this-day-in-history/heavens-gate-cult-members-found-dead

Editors, I. S. (2006). Heaven's Gate. Retrieved December 25, 2020, from https://infosect.freeshell.org/infocult/phenomene/English/HTML/doc0009.htm

Editors, P. W. (1976, November). THE 17 STEPS - Behavioral guidelines given in the early days of the classroom. Retrieved December 25, 2020, from https://www.psywww.com/psyrelig/hg/2-5.htm

Editors, T. T. (2005, October 1). Cult's views shaped by leader's shame. Retrieved December 25, 2020, from https://www.tampabay.com/archive/1997/03/29/cult-s-views-shaped-by-leader-s-shame/

Editors, T. W. (1997, April 16). The People's Voice: No. 21: Thanks for the Memories. Retrieved December 25, 2020, from https://tulsaworld.com/archive/the-peoples-voice-no-21-thanks-for-the-memories/article_03a7ef17-9524-570b-84ad-393bea39b5bb.html

Editors, V. P. (1997, March 29). CALIFORNIA CULT LEADER HAS VIRGINIA TIES HE STUDIED BRIEFLY AT RICHMOND'S UNION THEOLOGICAL SEMINARY IN 1952. Retrieved December 25, 2020, from https://scholar.lib.vt.edu/VA-news/VA-Pilot/issues/1997/vp970329/03290392.htm

Editors, W. (1997, March 27). Do and Ti's Long, Strange Trip Toward Death. Retrieved December 25, 2020, from https://www.wired.com/1997/03/do-and-tis-long-strange-trip-toward-death/

Editors, W. P. (1997, March 28). CULT LEADER RENOUNCED SEXUALITY. Retrieved December 25, 2020, from https://greensboro.com/cult-leader-renounced-sexuality/article_0d38f59f-75e7-5cba-9a18-da87ae8b1797.html

Egitto, D. (2020, April 20). Heaven's Gate Cult Members Keep The Faith After Infamous Mass Suicide. Retrieved December 25, 2020, from https://www.oxygen.com/deadly-cults/crime-news/heavens-gate-cult-still-believes-deadly-cults

Esculapio, A. (2018). CULT STATUS. Retrieved December 25, 2020, from http://vestoj.com/cult-status/

Ewing, E. (2018, January 31). Heaven 's Gate 's Website: The Group is Gone, the Religion Lives On. Retrieved December 25, 2020, from https://core.ac.uk/download/pdf/216862911.pdf

Ferrell, D., Katz, J., & Riccardi, N. (1997, March 30). Lives on the Fringe. Retrieved December 25, 2020, from https://www.latimes.com/archives/la-xpm-1997-03-30-mn-43664-story.html

Fisher, M., & Pressley, S. A. (1997, March 29). CRISIS OF SEXUALITY LAUNCHED STRANGE JOURNEY. Retrieved December 25, 2020, from https://www.washingtonpost.com/archive/politics/1997/03/29/crisis-of-sexuality-launched-strange-journey/3709d9ff-51ee-4f50-a9cd-a45525d7ad8f/

Fordahl, M. (1997, April 2). Bodies of cult members released as investigation winds down. Retrieved December 25, 2020, from https://apnews.com/article/05e883018d7e4a38d91b8fd1dee1bb89

Gallagher, J. (1997, April 6). Cult heard part of word heaven's gate showed esteem for the bible, selectively. Retrieved December 25, 2020, from https://www.baltimoresun.com/news/bs-xpm-1997-04-06-1997096004-story.html

Hafford, M. (2017, March 24). Heaven's Gate 20 Years Later: 10 Things You Didn't Know. Retrieved December 25, 2020, from https://www.rollingstone.com/feature/heavens-gate-20-years-later-10-things-you-didnt-know-114563/

Higgins, C. (2012, November 9). Stop Saying 'Drink the Kool-Aid'. Retrieved December 25, 2020, from https://www.theatlantic.com/health/archive/2012/11/stop-saying-drink-the-kool-aid/264957/

John, F. J. (2016, June 5). Spooky UFO cult lured away 20 Oregonians to follow "The Two". Retrieved December 25, 2020, from https://offbeatoregon.com/1606a.heavens-gate-ufo-cult-394.html

Koymasky, A. (2008, July 2). Marshall Herff Applewhite Jr. Retrieved December 25, 2020, from http://andrejkoymasky.com/liv/fam/bioa2/applew01.html

Lamoureux, A. (2020, December 6). THE UNTOLD TRUTH OF HEAVEN'S GATE. Retrieved December 25, 2020, from https://www.grunge.com/290309/the-untold-truth-of-heavens-gate/

Lattin, D. (2012, January 30). The Gospel According to Applewhite / A bit of Theosophy, a bit of X-Files, a bit from the Book of Revelation -- the mix-and-match theology of the Heaven's Gate cult had antecedents everywhere. Retrieved December 25, 2020, from https://www.sfgate.com/news/article/The-Gospel-According-to-Applewhite-A-bit-of-2847186.php

Lindlaw, S. (1997, March 29). Some male cult members, including leader, were castrated. Retrieved December 25, 2020, from https://apnews.com/article/fc9ffd3235d37830cf26da5ad1720b4d

Margaritoff, M. (2019, November 14). Marshall Applewhite And The Heaven's Gate Suicides. Retrieved December 25, 2020, from https://allthatsinteresting.com/cult-leaders/6

Martin, C. (2006, February 5). CU-Boulder prof formed madrigal group. Retrieved December 25, 2020, from https://www.denverpost.com/2006/02/05/cu-boulder-prof-formed-madrigal-group/

Martin, C. (2018, June 7). The seductive power of uniforms and cult dress codes. Retrieved December 25, 2020, from https://edition.cnn.com/style/article/seductive-power-of-uniforms-and-cult-dress/index.html

Melton, J. G. (2013, October 7). Heaven's Gate. Retrieved December 25, 2020, from https://www.britannica.com/topic/Heavens-Gate-religious-group#ref700331

Nakamura, R. (2020, December 2). Heaven's Gate Cult Member Explains in HBO Max Docuseries Why They All Wanted to Get Castrated (Exclusive Video). Retrieved December 25, 2020, from https://www.thewrap.com/heavens-gate-cult-member-explains-in-hbo-max-docuseries-why-they-all-wanted-to-get-castrated-exclusive-video/

Osnos, E. (2012, December 19). What's with the Chinese Mayan-Doomsday Cult? Retrieved December 25, 2020, from https://www.newyorker.com/news/evan-osnos/whats-with-the-chinese-mayan-doomsday-cult

Paul, A. (2015, March 24). Heaven's Gate Cult Members Might Eat Better Than You. Retrieved December 25, 2020, from https://www.vice.com/en/article/z4g7wa/heavens-gate-cult-members-might-eat-better-than-you

Reiher, A. (2017, November 2). American Horror Story: The Tragic Story Behind Marshall Applewhite and Heaven's Gate. Retrieved December 25, 2020, from https://www.yahoo.com/lifestyle/american-horror-story-tragic-story-030506978.html

Reimann, M. (2016, October 15). Suicide, Nikes, and comet space ships: The story of the Heaven's Gate cult. Retrieved December 25, 2020, from https://timeline.com/the-heavens-gate-mass-suicide-7f440ab4b333

Robinson, W. G. (1997, December 1). Heaven's Gate: The End. Retrieved December 25, 2020, from https://academic.oup.com/jcmc/article/3/3/JCMC334/4584381

Santich, K. (1997, June 8). AT THE GATES OF HEAVEN. Retrieved December 25, 2020, from https://www.orlandosentinel.com/news/os-xpm-1997-06-08-9706050500-story.html

Schodolski, V. J. (1997, March 31). AFTER EPIPHANY, EX-CULTIST SHADOWED HEAVEN'S GATE. Retrieved December 25, 2020, from https://www.chicagotribune.com/news/ct-xpm-1997-03-31-9703310072-story.html

Schwartz, O. (2020, January 9). My journey into the dark, hypnotic world of a millennial guru. Retrieved December 25, 2020, from https://www.theguardian.com/world/2020/jan/09/strange-hypnotic-world-millennial-guru-bentinho-massaro-youtube

Sledge, P. (2020, December 3). Heaven's Gate: The Cult Of Cults: 7 Things To Remember Before The HBO Docuseries. Retrieved December 25, 2020, from https://www.cinemablend.com/television/2559597/heavens-gate-the-cult-of-cults-7-things-to-remember-before-the-hbo-docuseries

St. Clair, J. (2020, December 4). What to Know About Heaven's Gate Cult Leader Marshall Applewhite. Retrieved December 25, 2020, from https://www.menshealth.com/entertainment/a34817569/marshall-applewhite-do-heavens-gate/

Staff, I. (2019, March 5). Do's "Transfiguration Diet". Retrieved December 25, 2020, from https://imgur.com/a/H6QltjJ

Steinberg, J. (1997, March 29). From Religious Childhood To Reins of a U.F.O. Cult. Retrieved December 25, 2020, from https://www.nytimes.com/1997/03/29/us/from-religious-childhood-to-reins-of-a-ufo-cult.html

Swain, S. (2019, April 15). Exclusive: Bizarre alien theories of Doomsday cult. Retrieved December 25, 2020, from https://www.9news.com.au/national/true-crime-news-cults-heavens-gate-supreme-truth-japan-usa/9539325f-ddb4-4368-b884-714a4ca07ad5

Taylor, M. (1997, May 20). Cult Survivor Thinks There's a Reason / Charles Humphrey says he may soon find out what it is. Retrieved December 25, 2020, from https://www.sfgate.com/news/article/Cult-Survivor-Thinks-There-s-a-Reason-Charles-2839141.php

Taylor, M. (1997, May 7). Another Heaven's Gate Suicide / Cultist found dead in Encinitas hotel. Retrieved December 25, 2020, from https://www.sfgate.com/news/article/Another-Heaven-s-Gate-Suicide-Cultist-found-2841156.php

Wicker, A. (2018, September 15). Nike & The Most Infamous Normcore Cult Suicide Of All Time. Retrieved December 25, 2020, from https://www.refinery29.com/en-us/heavens-gate-cult-nike-decades-reddit-story

Free Books by Charles River Editors

We have brand new titles available for free most days of the week. To see which of our titles are currently free, click on this link.

Discounted Books by Charles River Editors

We have titles at a discount price of just 99 cents everyday. To see which of our titles are currently 99 cents, click on this link.

www.ingramcontent.com/pod-product-compliance
Lightning Source LLC
Chambersburg PA
CBHW081937120726
47997CB00010B/3167